Andy,

It was worth the wait!

You are an artist and it was
such a pleasure having around for
us and Lucy!

Enjoy my last book - foxes next!

Lots of love,

x Matt

M Mann '20

HAMPSTEAD HEATH

London's Countryside

Matthew Maran

HEMISPHERE PUBLISHING, LONDON

[Page 1] A common tern banks left over the Men's Pond in search of fish, which it catches directly from the water. In summer, these birds can often be seen flying along the chain of Highgate Ponds.

[Pages 2–3] Light snowfall settles on the trees and shrubs around Viaduct Bridge.

[Pages 4–5] Take a stroll off the beaten path and there are hidden treasures to be found. In late April and early May bluebells carpet this patch of woodland in the centre of the Heath.

[Pages 6–7] Picnics are hugely popular on Hampstead Heath in the summer time. The open meadows and wonderful city views make it a favourite place for many who come to relax and enjoy nature.

[Pages 8–9] Looking across Bird Bridge with Viaduct Bridge in the background. Tens of thousands of deciduous trees on the Heath produce a spectacular show of colour in autumn.

[Page 14] A kestel launches from an oak tree in Cohen's Fields. These small birds of prey can be seen hunting over the Heath's grasslands.

Hampstead Heath, London's Countryside

First published in 2016
by Hemisphere Publishing
hemispherepublishing.com

Copyright © 2016 Matthew Maran Ltd
matthewmaran.com

Words and photographs by Matthew Maran
Designed by Matthew Maran and Al Newman – alnewmandesign.com
Book production by David Brimble – davidbrimble.com
Edited by Al Newman, Steven Swaby, Adrian Brooker and Vicki Vrint
Colour reproduction by DawkinsColour Ltd – dawkinscolour.co.uk
Printed and bound in Italy by Printer Trento

All photographs taken with permission of the City of London Corporation
Photographs taken on the Kenwood Estate with permission of English Heritage
Map on pages 20–21 reproduced by permission of the National Library of Scotland
Photograph of Matthew Maran on dust jacket by Adrian Brooker

ISBN 978-0-9568196-2-8

A catalogue record of this book is available from the British Library

CONTENTS

FOREWORD

I have always had a keen attachment to Hampstead Heath. I was brought up in London and spent many years going to Regent's Park as it was near to where my grandmother lived. By the time I was 17 I had started my three-year drama course in Chalk Farm and many of us lived in 'digs' near the Heath, where we would go to learn our lines. I loved the wind blowing the pages of the script, challenging me to concentrate all the more. Since those early years I have always enjoyed a love affair with nature, as if nature itself was part of my process of becoming an actor.

We were sent religiously to London Zoo to study the behaviour of animals and their movements. When I add those years up I realise how many had been spent in either Regent's Park or Hampstead Heath, and Holland Park too, where I rented for a while and where I used to take my daughter Tammy when she was a baby. When my son Josh was little it was obvious he was going to be involved in all things to do with nature. He is now a conservationist and through him I became a member of Fauna and Flora International.

I first met Matt when Josh and he became fast friends in their teens. I was there in London 15 years ago, when they were about to embark on a year-long trip across Africa in a second-hand Land Rover to study the wildlife. Josh creosoted a storage box for the beloved vehicle in my front room while I stitched the curtains for the windows. Matt was the principal photographer and when they returned with a vast array of slides we, their family and friends, were awestruck.

The book you are holding, more than a decade on and with newer technology to hand, is no less extraordinary. He shows us a world of life and colours we have rarely seen and London wildlife we barely knew existed.

Matt saved scrupulously for his state-of-the-art camera, but of course it's the photographer's talent and his astonishing patience (in the long and often freezing wait for the right shot) that gives us the story as it is – from a veteran oak tree still standing proud, impervious to all weathers, to a kestrel on the wing, to the subtle shades of a new spring flower – all shot in a haze of light and dark, shadows and sunlight.

You feel, at least I do, as if you were there at the moment a particular photograph was taken, and you can sense the colours are fleeting and ever changing. Go back another day and the colours and shapes have transformed.

Photographs, the best ones, often invite us to explore the unknown, of worlds miles away. But in Matt's amazing pictures of the Heath, he shows us a hidden world in north London's very own 'countryside'. Aren't we lucky!

— Frances de la Tour

A WORD FROM THE CITY OF LONDON CORPORATION

It is a great privilege for the City of London Corporation to manage Hampstead Heath and we do so with landscape and nature conservation as our guiding stars. Busy in the machinations of management, we don't always have the time to sit back and appreciate the raw beauty of the plants and animals that we are striving to protect. It is, then, a great joy that Matthew Maran's stunning photographic record of the Heath's wildlife allows us to do so in jaw-dropping detail. We very much welcome this powerful contribution to the treasure trove of art and literature that has been inspired by Hampstead Heath.

The Heath is so much more than a park. It is a piece of countryside encapsulated within the city. It supports important populations of plants and animals including grass snakes in their closest colony to the centre of London, nine species of bat, breeding kingfishers and around 800 veteran trees. It is a place where Londoners can see wildlife up-close in a way that is often not possible in our intensively farmed rural landscape.

We often ask visitors what we can do to improve Hampstead Heath. The overwhelming response is along the lines of 'nothing, just keep it just as it is now!' But to retain the status quo we have to keep managing. To stop active management would be disastrous for the Heath. Without grassland management, our meadows would be lost to scrub and woodland within a generation. Without hedgerow management our hedges would become 'gappy' and unattractive to breeding birds. Without wetland management our ponds and lakes would ultimately silt up. Without woodland management, our sunny woodland glades would disappear.

Our job is to protect the wildlife value of Hampstead Heath. Wildflower meadow creation, hedge-laying, scientific monitoring, control of invasive species and reedbed planting are just a few of the techniques employed in that respect.

We also strive to provide Londoners with access to wildlife that will be enjoyable and will stimulate interest and knowledge. We run educational programmes that provide contact with nature, something that is not always easy for Londoners to find. Matthew's stunning book will undoubtedly enthuse anyone who reads it and for that reason alone we wholeheartedly welcome its publication.

— David Bentley, City of London Corporation

On a chilly November morning, mist gathers over Cohen's Fields before dawn.

INTRODUCTION

Over 800 veteran trees, more than 650 flowering plants, over 100 species of birds, 20 mammals and thousands of insect species have been recorded on Hampstead Heath, making it an outstanding national resource so close to the centre of a major world city. The Heath spans almost 800 acres of recent and ancient woodland, wildflower meadows and vast grassland slopes as well as over 30 ponds, large and small. Located in north London, five kilometres from the city centre, this magnificent green space is also a sanctuary for humans. Seven million people visit every year to run, walk dogs, swim in the ponds, have a picnic or simply sit on a bench and take in the spectacular views.

Present-day Hampstead Heath gives a sense of a past wilderness and it's easy to get lost in the fields and woodlands. Over the centuries the Heath has gone through many transformations. Archaeological digs reveal that people were using the land here as early as the Stone Age. Later, in medieval times, part of the area became a common on the edge of London for the villagers of Hampstead, where it was used for grazing and the gathering of wood for fuel. With changes in land ownership and urban development, the Heath changed further still down the years. In the late nineteenth century quarries were opened to extract

sand for building construction; the evidence is still there today in the hollows and pools of Sandy Heath in the north-western part of the Heath.

In the late eighteenth and early nineteenth centuries Hampstead Heath became a popular destination for people seeking recreation, a place to take a break from the hustle and bustle of the city. The damming of the Highgate and Hampstead brooks created the string of ponds on the Heath, which supplied some of London's water. The ponds soon became fashionable spas for the city's well-to-do.

Thanks to many dedicated individuals, visionary campaign groups and management bodies, the Heath has grown from a 200-acre common to 800 acres of beautiful and diverse habitat. In 1988 the area was made a Site of Metropolitan Importance for Nature Conservation, in recognition of its importance to wildlife in the city, and to the millions of people who visit each year to reconnect with nature. This book is a celebration of one of the most beautiful urban green spaces in the world. It is a special place. For some of us it is a sacred place.

Views of the city and surrounding area are spectacular from the top of Parliament Hill. One of the highest places in London it is also known as Kite Hill as crosswinds and the absence of tall trees make it ideal for kite flying.

A map showing Hampstead and part of the Heath in 1870, one year before it was sold to the Metropolitan Board of Works. The Hampstead Heath Act of 1871 states that 'The Board shall forever keep the Heath open, unenclosed and unbuilt on. The Board shall at all times preserve, as far as may be, the natural aspect and state of the Heath, and to that end shall protect the turf, gorse, heather, timber and other trees, shrubs and brushwood thereon.'

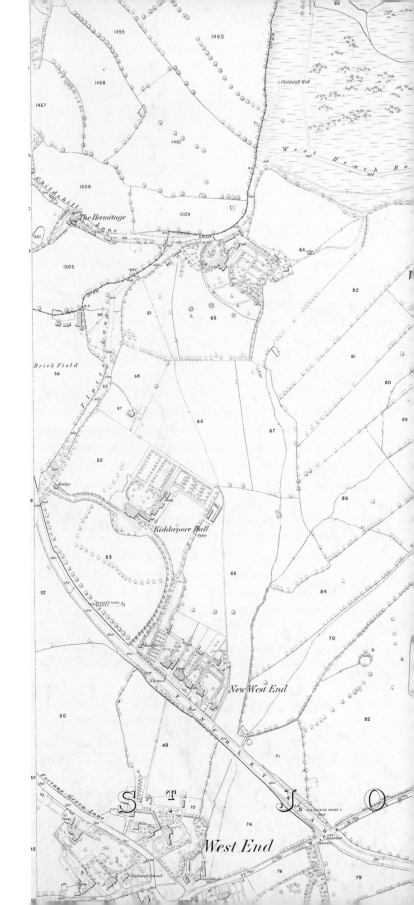

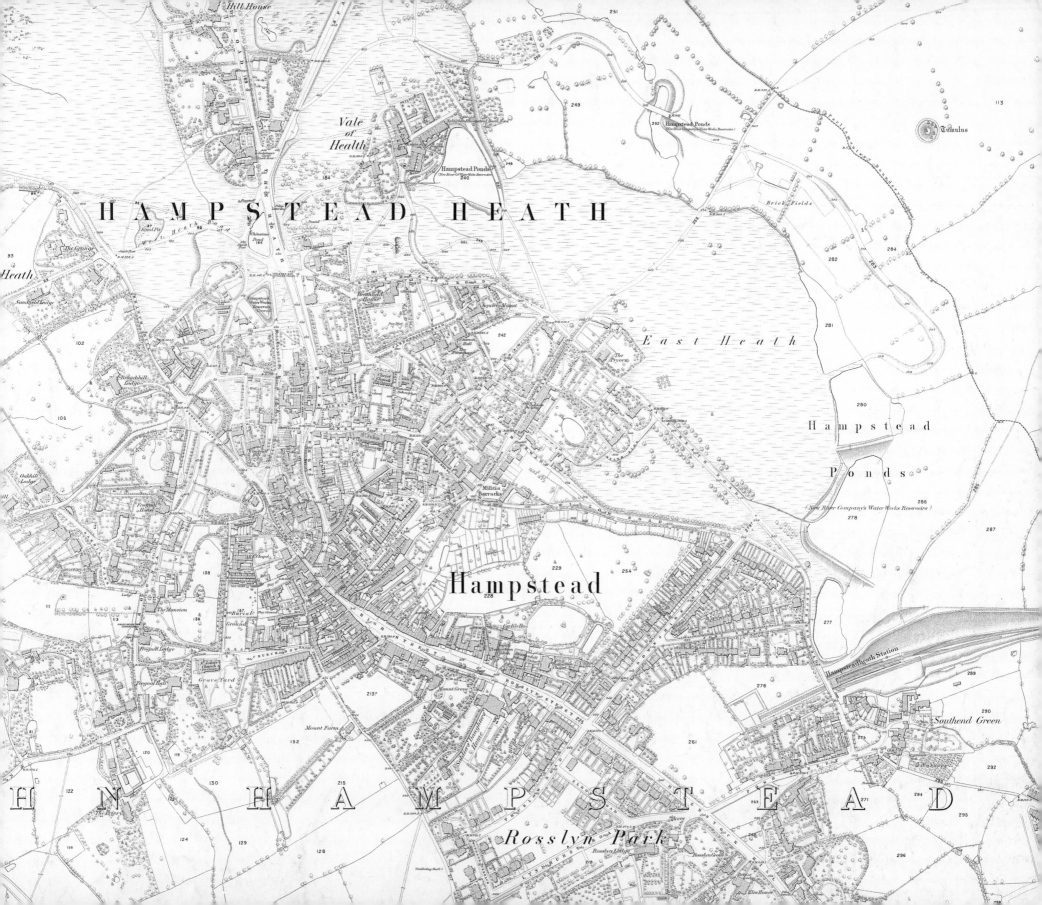

WINTER

After heavy snowfall, travelling in London can be difficult, particularly when attempting to reach the higher ground around Hampstead Heath. On arriving, thick snow covers the dramatic landscape in a soft blanket of silence. It's as if you've entered another world. For many, snowfall is an unwelcome disruption of daily life, but for regular visitors to the Heath it's an exciting time – a winter wonderland in the heart of the city.

Every season brings its own delights. Fresh green leaves and a wide variety of flowers in spring, warmth and long evenings during the summer, the rich colours and deep blue skies of autumn. Winter is extra special as it brings the possibility of snow, but a photographer must work quickly to capture images at this time because settling snow in London is usually short-lived.

Hampstead Heath is home to some magnificent oak trees. Here, the warm sunshine picks out the rich texture of the bark of this huge oak. The snowfall neatly covers each branch, highlighting the shape and form of the tree, helping it to stand out against the busy woodland background.

Snowy conditions offer a great chance to 'see' in black and white (a format often overlooked since the digital revolution). The scenery appears monochromatic, encouraging the photographer to think in tone rather than colour.

[Left] Robins are common on the Heath. Their boldness means it is relatively easy to get close to them, which is useful in photography when trying to capture intimate portraits. The birds move so fast I relied on my camera's shooting rate of eight-and-a-half frames per second and a little bit of luck to capture this action shot.

[Right] During the winter, a number of birds gather on the aptly named Bird Bridge at the centre of Hampstead Heath. It's a great location to watch robins and other species squabble over bird seed left by visitors. Here, positioning the lens low in order to get a 'robin's-eye view' helps to isolate the subject against the clean background.

[Previous spread] A carrion crow perches on a snow-covered fallen tree trunk. These highly intelligent birds can be seen all over the Heath, many of them gathering to roost west of Kenwood House.

[Left] A runner takes a short-cut through the mighty 'beeches' woodland. Running on the Heath is a great way to experience the endless trails off the beaten path.

Photography is a wonderful way to engage with nature, helping the practitioner to become more aware of shapes, tone and contrast, and to notice things that might otherwise have been missed. Hours can pass when focusing on a single subject and at times it can be a meditative process. It's easy to get lost in the detail of a wildflower or when studying the elements that compose a wide-angle landscape image.

The biggest challenge comes when attempting to capture with a camera what is seen with the naked eye. Making the image appear three-dimensional is something many photographers strive to achieve by including foreground detail, yet leaving enough space to draw the viewer into the image. The most powerful images are often those with the simplest compositions. A well-exposed, sharp frame with good light also needs to be considered.

This standing dead oak tree, a well-known feature in the fields close to the Highgate Ponds, adds interest and helps to balance the composition of this photograph. The horizon was clear enough to capture the setting sun before it dipped below the tree line.

[Left] This tree-lined avenue, situated along the path close to Kenwood House, takes on a different feel when it snows.

[Page 36] A black-headed gull swoops down from above, captured using a wide-angle lens, a slow shutter speed and a little fill-flash to freeze the action.

[Page 37, from top left] Redwings are difficult birds to get close to and a 1.4 teleconverter on a 300mm lens came in handy for this photograph, close to the eastern gate of Kenwood; A nuthatch's chestnut-brown sides and black stripe across its face make it easy to identify; A stonechat in Pryors Field; One of the UK's smallest birds, the goldcrest's bright yellow crest stands out on an overcast day.

Winter is an exciting time to photograph resident and migratory birds on the Heath. Finding enough food to see them through this cold period means birds are active and in many ways it's easier to spot them as there is little cover provided by the predominantly deciduous forest. Nuthatches, robins and goldcrests can be seen foraging in the woodlands, black-headed gulls congregate in large numbers on the Highgate chain of ponds and redwings are found roaming along the Heath's hedgerows, feeding on berries and searching for worms on the ground.

The diverse landscape and the spectacular vantage point over the city make the Heath a great place for bird watching in London. From the familiar to the rare you never quite know what may appear.

[Right] Mandarin ducks are native to East Asia but have established a feral population in the UK after escaping from captivity. They can be seen on many Heath ponds and sometimes in large numbers on the Stock Pond. The male's bright plumage adds a splash of colour to a dull winter's day.

[Overleaf] A veteran oak tree thought to be more than 300 years old stands hidden away south-east of the Kenwood Estate. The misty winter morning gave this picture atmosphere and a clean backdrop, enabling the old branches to stand out.

[Pages 42–43] Dog walkers are framed by the copper beech in the fields close to Highgate Ponds.

[Pages 44–47] Mist, a scattering of trees and the absence of people give a sense of the Heath's countryside feel.

[Left] Local swimmer Oliver Perritt prepares himself for a dawn dive at the Men's Pond. A group of committed swimmers take the plunge here all year round, unfazed by the icy winter waters.

Mei Tek Yeh has been visiting the Heath every day for more than 30 years. She lives a few minutes' walk from South End Green and feeds her favourite birds with a variety of seeds. You will probably hear Mei before you see her. Over the years she's developed a way of calling to the birds that they seem to understand. Great tits, blue tits, nuthatches and robins are among the species that swoop down hoping to grab a nut or seed, particularly during the winter when food is scarce. The birds forage for themselves in the spring and summer months but Mei still comes to the Heath every day. 'I used to love walking here with my dog but after he died it didn't stop me, I kept coming and I can now spend more time watching the birds, which gives me so much pleasure.'

[Left] Over many months Mei gained trust of a robin which feeds on meal worms directly from her hand, seen here on the path between Lime Avenue and Viaduct Bridge.

[Overleaf] This row of predominantly oak is an old lapsed field boundary on the Heath Extension. The boundary, which can be dated back to more than 300 years, used to divide Hill Field and Cart Path Field.

The view of the city from Parliament Hill, at the southern edge of Hampstead Heath, is protected by law. It is a popular place to watch both sunset and sunrise, making it one of the most visited locations on the Heath. Legend has it that Guy Fawkes planned to come here to witness his attempt to blow-up the Houses of Parliament in 1605.

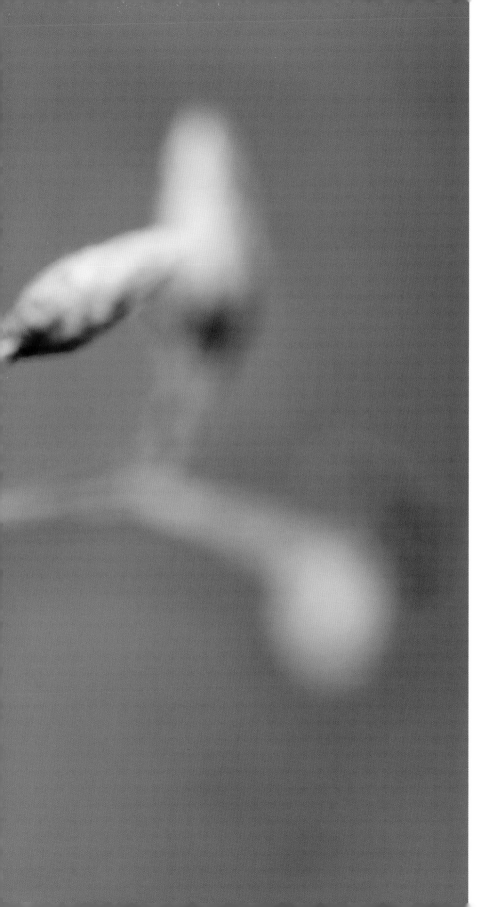

SPRING

It is sometimes easy to forget how short-lived the seasons are. Just as you begin to get used to a certain temperature and where the light falls at a certain time, a change can be sensed in the air that brings one season to an end and a new scent indicates the beginning of the next.

The British people are well known for discussing the weather and have good reason to because it is so changeable. This unpredictability is an opportunity for varied landscape photography as it's never certain when dramatic light will occur. A dull, drizzly day can often be the best time to get out with a camera and with lighter evenings and warmer temperatures, spring is a great time to shake off the winter blues.

[Left] A hornbeam leaf bud, soon to open, signifies the onset of spring.

[Overleaf] This dramatic sunset over Parliament Hill lasted just four minutes but underwent amazing changes in colour.

A dog walker enjoys a
misty morning by the
Model Boating Pond
in early spring.

It's always worth the effort
to make an early start and
dawn is a special time to be
up and about on the Heath.
This picture, looking east
towards St Michael's Church
in Highgate Village, was taken
just before sunrise.

[Left] Cascades of white flowers emerge before the leaves of a blackthorn bush on the Heath Extension.

[Overleaf] Spring daffodils adjacent to Kenwood House. Damp grey days are great for photographing colourful flowers. The cloud cover acts as a giant diffuser filter, preventing distracting highlights and shadows. The even light brings out detail, while moisture helps to saturate the colours.

[Left] A rose-ringed parakeet peeps out of an oak tree cavity. The UK's first naturalised parrot divides opinion – some find it a joy to watch a tropical green bird flying and squawking overhead, others see them as a potential threat to native birds as they compete for nest holes.

[Right] Sphagnum moss is rare in Greater London and where it exists the landscape is often carefully managed to ensure its survival. Sphagnum is associated with bogs, a wetland habitat that was once widespread across the country. Since the eighteenth century, bogs have decreased due to urban development and extraction of water. As the moss breaks down over many years peat is formed, which has been widely used for fuel and garden cultivation. The two sites where sphagnum is found closest to the centre of London are West Heath and the Kenwood Estate.

[Left] A female kestrel at Denzil's Copse, a ring of seven oak trees planted in memory of Denzil Budgett-Meakin, one of the founding members of the Highgate Society, a group that helps protect the Heath from urban development. Observed over a number of days, the kestrel was brought mice by a male and in-between visits would hunt for worms from the low branches.

[Right] Wings outstretched, a hunting kestrel hovers over Cohen's Fields.

[Previous spread] It takes time to learn how to identify different species, with form, behaviour and habitat all coming into play. Here it was only as I got closer to the tree that I noticed the unmistakeable shape of a bird of prey. I couldn't believe my luck. The kestrel paused momentarily allowing me to frame it with the Shard in the distance before flying off to a neighbouring field.

[Right] A macro lens offers an alternative perspective of a cow parsley flower. This common perennial plant is found all over the Heath in meadows and at the edges of hedgerows and woodland.

[Overleaf] A selection of flowers that can be seen on the Heath in spring. [Left page, from top left] Dandelion; buttercup; apple; bluebells; cuckoo; pignut; cowslip; hawthorn; horse chestnut. [Overleaf, right page, from top left] Common sorrel; bush vetch; bramble; red campion; wild service; elder; gorse; nettle; red clover.

Mute swans are one of
Britain's largest birds,
reaching a height of over
one-and-a-half metres, with
a wingspan of up to three
metres. They can be seen
on both the Highgate and
Hampstead chain of ponds.

Sunsets can be dramatic on
a cloudy day, as seen here,
reflected in the waters of
Hampstead No. 2 Pond. Using
a flashgun to highlight the
plumage of two passing drake
mallards added extra colour to
the composition.

[Left] Two veteran beech trees grow side by side close to Springett's Wood. The ground beneath these trees turns a magnificent colour in autumn as their huge canopies shed thousands of leaves.

[Right] The beginning of the River Fleet winds through the Stock Pond in early spring. The Fleet is the capital's largest lost river and was once an important source for potable water for the City of London. It also provided power, transport and was used as a sewer. The Fleet originates on Hampstead Heath and small streams are still evident today.

[Left] Green woodpeckers can be seen feeding on ant nests in the open fields. Their countershaded green backs and light undersides provide excellent camouflage in the grasslands, yet they can be easily identified by their loud laugh-like call and undulating flight pattern. Getting close to these shy birds is difficult as their ground-feeding behaviour leaves them vulnerable to predators, meaning they are constantly on the lookout. The green woodpecker's long tongue, at approximately 10cm, allows it to probe into nests to feed on ants and their larvae.

[Right] A green woodpecker shows off its beautiful plumage in flight. They can be seen year-round across the Heath in open meadows such as Cohen's and Pryors Fields.

As the seasons change there is a short window of mixed weather that presents magnificent photo opportunities. This is a great time to photograph the Heath, especially if heavy rain is forecast. Breaks in the clouds allow the sun to burst through momentarily and create dramatic skies.

[Right] White pignut and crimson common sorrel cover much of Cohen's Fields and Ladies' Pond Meadow during the spring and summer months. Open fields such as this make up a large part of the Heath, providing a habitat for invertebrates and birds, as well as a picturesque picnic spot.

[Overleaf] A wild service tree in full bloom at the edge of Cohen's Fields. There are 19 mature wild service trees on the Heath, nine of which are situated on the Kenwood Estate. Recognised as an ancient woodland indicator species, it is often found in old hedgerows and is one of the UK's rarer native trees.

[Pages 92–93] Enter the Heath from Hampstead Lane and this amazing view of the London skyline presents itself. Capturing this image required use of the City of London's tree officers' MEWP (Mobile Elevated Working Platform), also called a 'cherry picker', in order to gain a higher vantage point over the fresh green canopy.

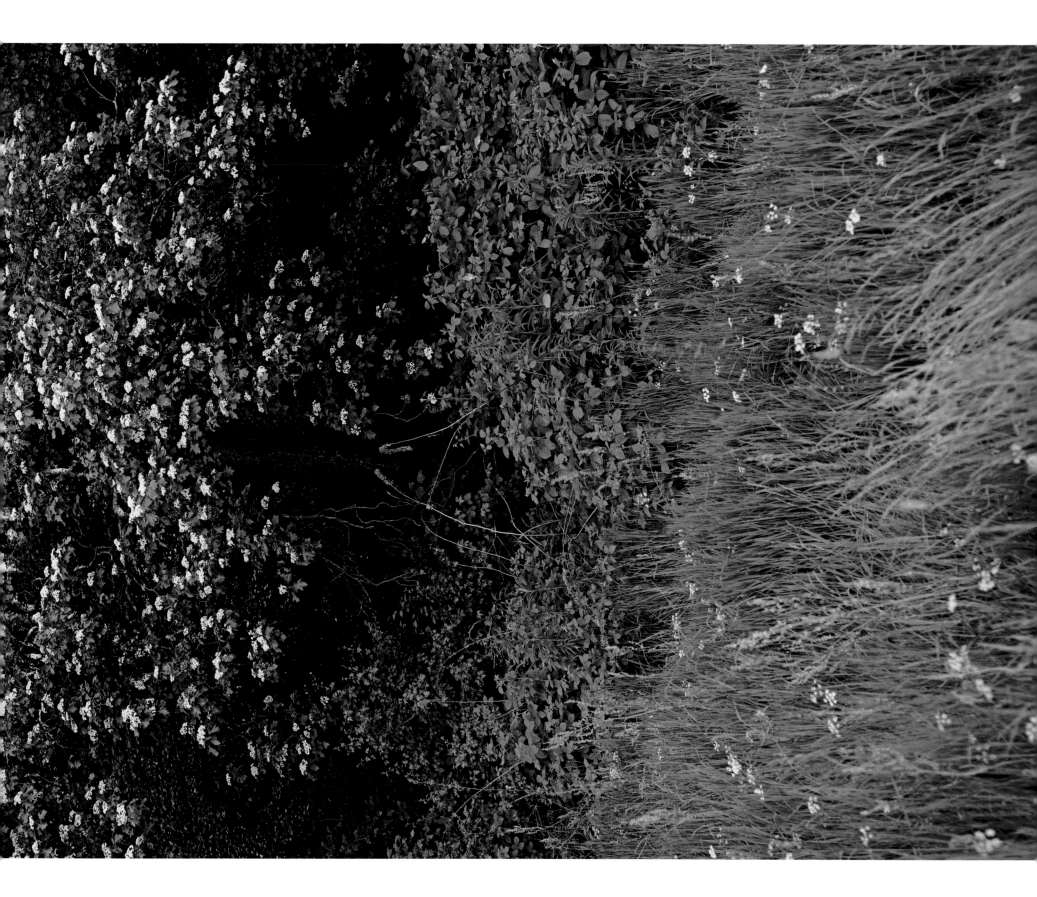

SUMMER

The Heath teems with visitors in the summer months yet its vastness means it is still possible to find a secluded spot and take a break from busy city life. It's also a place for adventure – a swim in the ponds, a game of frisbee or a run in the cool evening, are just a few of a long list of activities that draw people here.

It's a busy time for wildlife too, with animals attracted to the Heath for its feeding opportunities. Bees visit the numerous wildflowers that cover the open fields, kestrels hunt rodents in the tall grass at the woodland edge and hedgehogs forage at night for insects in the undergrowth.

This time of year best showcases the wide range of habitats present on the Heath, which explode into life with the warm temperatures and long days. Acid grasslands, hedgerows, recent and ancient woodland, wetlands and scrub all support numerous plant and animal species.

Just after sunrise a runner takes advantage of the cooler morning temperatures on a midsummer's day by the Model Boating Pond.

It's hard to believe the Heath is just five kilometres from central London when taking a dip in one of its three swimming ponds. Two of these are open year round and provide a unique opportunity to engage with nature. For the fair-weather swimmer this might be a refreshing dip in the July sunshine, while for a small group of hardcore swimmers it could mean braving the freezing cold on a January morning.

In the summer months swimmers are joined by cormorants, grey herons, coots, kingfishers, moorhens, gulls and more, which come to hunt fish and feed on the aquatic plants. Mallards rest on lifebuoys, common terns dive for meals between swimmers and great crested grebes build nests at the water's edge.

[Left] Head lifeguard Terry Turner has worked at the Heath's ponds for more than 30 years. When asked what has kept him there for so long, his response is simple: 'Look at it, it's beautiful.'

[Overleaf] Year-round swimmer Martin Pate is in the right place at the right time for this picture as a grebe parent and its chick swim past.

The great crested grebe was almost hunted to extinction in the UK for its striking plumage, which was used to decorate hats in Victorian times. Through conservation efforts it has recovered well and today there are over 5,000 breeding pairs. It also has a wide global distribution across most of Europe, Asia and parts of Africa and Australasia. It breeds successfully on both the Highgate and Hampstead chain of ponds, adapting well to the urban environment.

When eggs are laid great crested grebes share incubating duties and for the first few days of its life the stripy chick rides on the parent's back. Their diet consists mainly of fish, but they also eat insects and small frogs.

Getting into the water in a wetsuit allows observation of grebe feeding behaviour at their level, here catching prey such as a passing mayfly [left] and a perch [right].

Non-native red swamp crayfish, originating from south-eastern America, were first recorded in the UK on Hampstead Heath in 1991. Part kept in-check by grebes and part by the Heath's conservation team this invasive species is difficult to manage and can disrupt the pond ecosystem. Here a grebe catches a crayfish, thrashing it on the water's surface to subdue it before swallowing it whole.

Common terns are widely distributed across Europe, Asia and North America. In the UK they are found predominantly along the coast and at a variety of inland habitats including lakes and marshes. A pair of terns can often be seen hunting on the Highgate Ponds, frequently hovering over water before plunge-diving to catch fish. They leave in October, migrating to West Africa where they spend the winter.

Visitors to the Men's Pond will be familiar with these birds as they show little fear around humans, sometimes diving in-between swimmers. Adult terns work tirelessly, hunting prey to feed their chicks who call noisily when a parent flies overhead, hoping for a fresh catch.

[Previous spread] A tern prepares to land after a hunt. A tripod, remote trigger and wide-angle lens allowed for this close-up shot.

[Above, left] Terns are noisy birds, particularly when feeding. Their loud call is like an audio cue for the arrival of one of the parents, which is useful in anticipating and capturing a range of behaviour shots.

[Above, right] A tern surveys the water for potential prey. They typically dive from a height of one to five metres to catch fish.

[Right] A parent delivers a meal to its young and returns to hunt for more without landing.

[Left] A macro lens can allow the viewer to see detail that the naked eye cannot.

[Right] A field of oxeye daisies bursts into life close to the bandstand in Parliament Hill Fields. The overcast day provides even lighting, which is ideal when photographing white flowers. This large patch established itself just two years after being planted and supports a variety of wildlife.

[Overleaf] A spread of buttercups in the evening sun on Cohen's Fields.

[Previous spread] A selection of flowers that can be seen on the Heath in summer. [Left page, from top left] Small balsam; dog rose; meadow cranesbill; cat's ear; Russian comfrey; tormentil; musk marrow; American willowherb; herb robert. [Previous spread, right page, from top left] Heath bedstraw; yellow crucifer; purple-loosestrife; foxglove; yarrow; lesser stitchwort; green alkanet; white clover; common ragwort.

[Left] A selection of grasses that can be seen on the Heath. [From left] Meadow foxtail; red fescue; cocksfoot; Yorkshire fog; common reed.

115

[Left] A common blue butterfly visits a heather flower in a clearing on Sandy Heath. The UK has a significant proportion of the north-western lowland heathland. Lowland heathland develops on impoverished soils and with few exceptions has been sustained by human intervention, in some cases going back 6,000 years. This habitat was once widespread here and indeed gave the Heath its name.

[Right] A meadow brown momentarily rests on grass in Cohen's Fields. Butterflies thrive on the Heath's open grasslands. A wide variety of wildflowers support many species in the spring and summer. The Heath has one of the oldest butterfly recording schemes in the country, and 23 different species have been recorded here.

Cohen's Fields are prime hunting grounds for Heath predators. Here, a common blue damselfly [left] grapples with a moth in the dry summer grass while a kestrel [above] hovers over the fields, surveying the ground for mice and other prey.

There are many reasons people come to the Heath. Some locals enjoy the peace at dawn when no one else is around. Others travel from further afield for a cup of tea in the café at Kenwood House, catching the last rays of the setting sun while reading the local papers.

Any visitor to the Heath will almost certainly cross paths with a runner. Whether it's for short sprints and hill-reps up Parliament Hill or longer runs across the fields and secluded woodland trails, many running and other outdoor activity groups use the Heath as a training ground.

Dog walkers, runners, swimmers, bird watchers, wildflower enthusiasts, picnickers... the list is endless. The Heath has something for everyone.

Flat ground is hard to come by on the Heath but the reward for getting to the top of a steep hill is another spectacular view of the London skyline.

[Above left] The many stages of blackberry fruit. They turn from green to red before they are ripe, and black when they are at their most succulent.

[Above right] Blackberry picking is a popular pastime in late summer but it's not only humans that benefit from this plant's abundance on the Heath. Caterpillars and small mammals use them for food and they are a great source of energy for soon-to-depart migrant birds. The thorny stems also provide great protection against predators.

[Right] A prize blackberry worth reaching high for.

Cohen's Fields is one
of many open areas on
the Heath perfect for a
game of frisbee.

An essential part of Hampstead Heath's management plan is to protect and enhance populations of plants and animals. A recent report revealed a small but widespread population of grass snakes, prompting ecologist Adrian Brooker, along with a team of trained and committed volunteers, to develop a snake monitoring programme. Snakes like to rest in warm places during the day, so 'snake mats' – thick, black pieces of material the size of a doormat which warm up quickly and retain heat – are left out in fenced-off areas around the Heath. A brief look beneath the mats is an easy way to monitor the population with minimal impact.

Habitat improvement works including the creation of new ponds to increase populations of amphibians such as frogs and newts (the snake's main source of food) have also taken place. Snake numbers have been seen to increase since improvement works began and it is not uncommon to see 15 individual snakes on a single monitoring trip.

Conservation areas such as the Bird Sanctuary provide habitats, free from disturbance from visitors and dogs, allowing many plants and animals to thrive.

[Left] Snakes don't have eyelids but instead have a transparent layer over the eye called the brille, which helps protect against dust and dirt. This layer turns a milky white colour before moulting and the brille is also shed along with the skin.

[Right] A snake's tongue has many uses. By picking up particles from the air they can taste, smell and detect prey.

In 2015, the City of London ecologists began a pilot project to monitor hedgehog populations in Golders Hill Park, in the west of the Heath. Individuals were weighed, sexed and tagged before being released. Golders Hill Park is one of the few places on Hampstead Heath that is locked at night and it appears that hedgehogs thrive here as a result. The size of the current population is unknown but with a new monitoring and volunteer programme in place and careful habitat management it is hoped that numbers will increase for this much-loved mammal.

[Left] Hedgehogs are primarily nocturnal mammals. They are omnivorous: their diet consists of insects, snails, grass roots and mushrooms. They hibernate in winter, when their body temperature can drop as low as 2° Celsius.

[Right] A hedgehog's best defence is to curl up and rely on its thorny spines for protection. Although this work intrudes a little into the lives of the hedgehogs the data collected is vital to help ecologists learn more about their behaviour and habitat, in order to educate volunteers and the wider public to protect them in the future.

A kingfisher sighting on the Heath is usually a fleeting glimpse – a flash of darting blue and the sound of a shrill whistle. These birds have a transparent third eyelid to help them see underwater when catching fish. Different kingfisher species can be found in varied habitat zones all around the world, from coasts, rivers and forests to mountains. Not all of them specialise in eating fish – some have a varied diet that includes arthropods, amphibians, reptiles, and even small birds.

A man-made kingfisher bank has existed on the far side of the Bird Sanctuary next to the Model Boating Pond for more than 20 years. Over the past ten years there have been regular sightings of breeding pairs using the bank as their home and to raise young.

[Left] A kingfisher emerges from the water after diving in for a wash. Their nests, in the side of the bank, are messy places full of mud and fish bones and the adults must keep their feathers in good condition in order to catch enough fish to feed their young.

[Above] Landing on a branch with a freshly caught fish in its beak, an adult kingfisher prepares to enter the nest to feed its young. To capture these images a temporary hide was erected with permission from the ecologists. Over a two week period and more than 30 hours spent in the hide there were only a couple of occasions when the light was strong enough to penetrate the thick vegetation and illuminate the bird's striking plumage.

{Overleaf} A large patch of purple-loosestrife comes into bloom in August at the Bird Sanctuary.

A green city such as London provides important habitats for bees. Here they are less exposed to pesticides and herbicides than in parts of the countryside and have access to a wide variety of flowering plants in parks and back gardens. Bees are vitally important for pollinating hundreds of plant species and many of the crops we eat. The Heath's wildflower meadows provide prime habitat for a number of bee species and other invertebrates that hunt, feed and shelter in the tall grasses.

[Left] A white-tailed bumblebee visits a black knapweed flower in Cohen's Fields near the Hampstead Lane entrance.

[Right] A honey bee flies towards a purple-loosestrife flower in the Bird Sanctuary.

[Overleaf] A hidden gem on Hampstead Heath, the Pergola is a spectacular raised walkway with wonderful views over West Heath. It can be visited year round and is at its most beautiful in the spring and summer, when an array of climbing plants burst into life, twist up the columns and cover the gnarly twisted beams.

[Previous spread] Two Tree Hill is a significant landmark of Sandy Heath. Sand was excavated here in the late nineteenth century and evidence of these works is apparent today in the hollows and mounds covering the area. Early records show an almost treeless landscape apart from these two veteran oaks. Old metalwork can still be seen lodged high in the canopy, which may have provided a pulley system for moving bags of sand. Additionally the mound that these two trees sit on is a special study site for mycorrhizal fungi as it is surrounded by a fence and has been largely undisturbed.

[Right] The 'super moon' that occurred in late September 2015 rises over Parliament Hill Fields.

AUTUMN

As you walk from the open fields into the woodland you move from one world into another. The temperature cools, the light softens and the quiet world of the woodland gathers you into its stillness. Standing among veteran trees that have lived for hundreds of years can be a meditative experience.

With so many deciduous trees, the Heath's woodlands are transformed in the autumn with a beautiful display of crimson red, ochre yellow and rich browns. Photographing in this setting requires a different mentality and skill set from the fast reactions and often frantic shooting needed to capture much of the Heath's wildlife. In the woods the pace is slower and the opportunities for great photographs are endless. Mosses and lichens nestle in the bark of oaks and beech trees, weird and wonderful fungi colonise dead wood and a network of gnarly roots and fallen leaves covers the ground.

There are incredible specimens of old-growth beech, oak and wild service trees. Many of these trees are survivors from ancient hedgerows, planted as field boundaries to demarcate land ownership. Considering how much the urban landscape has changed and continues to change in London, it feels like a privilege to stand among trees that are centuries old.

Old-growth beech trees in the woodlands in the central area of the Heath. There is something magical about being surrounded by these veteran trees. Simplifying the composition and leaving space for the picture to breathe can help convey that experience into an image.

[Left] This photograph was taken from inside a hollow but living tree, known locally as 'Hollow beech'. The tree visible through the cavity is one of the Heath's few wild service trees. The tree and the old hedgeline it grows in once marked a parish boundary. The Heath is also home to the UK's tallest wild service tree.

[Right] The beech tree (left) appears to be pushed by the oak tree (right) as they compete for space. The growth could also be providing support for the oak. This natural phenomenon is known as inosculation, when contact through movement is made and stimulates natural grafting – it is more commonly seen in two trees of the same species.

With over 20,000 trees on Hampstead Heath the arboriculture team have a challenging task in managing the trees for safety, wildlife conservation, pests and disease. 'No two days are the same and with such a variety of trees, you get to see so much change throughout the year,' says trees management officer David Humphries. He and his team take a measured approach to their work. 'With so many trees you would think we get the chainsaws out every day but our method is a holistic one and learnt over a long period of time. We share our knowledge with other conservation arborists, students and the general public. The City of London is at the forefront of conservation arboriculture, not just on the Heath but at other sites such as Burnham Beeches and Epping Forest.'

[Above] Trees management officer David Humphries has been working on the Heath for more than 30 years and his knowledge and enthusiasm for the job are inspiring.

[Right] Arborist Conrad Daniels pauses for a portrait 30 metres up a veteran oak tree.

There are thought to be more than five million species of fungi in the world today, outnumbering plant species by more than six to one. Many remain to be discovered and it is estimated that 12,000 new species are discovered every year. The UK is home to more than 15,000 species, many of which can be found on the Heath.

Fungi are the principal decomposers in an ecosystem, playing an essential role in nutrient recycling. Without them, stacks of dead timber and organic matter would litter the ground, restricting access to the forests and fields.

[Right] Sulphur tuft nestles in the bark of a fallen oak tree. Using a small reflective panel helped to illuminate the fungi in the fading light beneath the dark canopy.

[Overleaf] A selection of fungi that can be seen on the Heath. [Left page, from top left] Common ink cap; zoned rosette; fly agaric; beefstake; oak mazegill; fluted bird's nest; clouded funnel; leafy brain; common puffball. [Overleaf, right page, from top left] Razor strop; red cracking bolete; lacquered bracket; brittlegill; hairy curtain crust; wrinkled peach; rigidoporus sp.; spectacular rustgill; death cap.

The distinctive red cap
of a fly agaric fungus in
Golders Hill Park. As when
photographing wildlife,
shooting from a low angle
can produce more engaging
photographs. Here, use of a
wide-angle lens shows more
of the mushroom's habitat.

153

[Right] Fallen branches on Sandy Heath are covered in hairy curtain crust, a common fungus with a vibrant orange colour and frilly edge.

[Overleaf] The iridescent porcelain fungus is associated with beech trees and can be seen on dead trunks, fallen branches and high up on dead wood. This one, close to Bird Bridge, was captured using a wide aperture to help it to stand out against the blurry autumnal background.

The Kenwood Estate sits on 74 acres of land managed separately by English Heritage. Situated along the northern boundary of the Heath it has a different feel to the more natural heath land. Kenwood House is a main attraction here and is home to a fine art collection including paintings by Turner, Gainsborough, Rembrandt and Vermeer.

Formally known as Caen Wood House, it dates back to the early seventeenth century; the ownership and layout of the house have changed many times since then. Much of the landscape design still present today is the creation of the celebrated landscape architect Humphry Repton, who carried out work here in the late eighteenth century.

The Kenwood landscape is more cultivated, with ornamental planting and lush sloping lawns. Yet around one third of the estate is a Site of Special Scientific Interest, mainly due to its ancient woodlands and the variety of wildlife it supports.

[Left] A rabbit pauses while grazing on the Kenwood Estate. They can be seen at dawn and dusk feeding on the lush green lawns.

[Right] Carrion crows roosting in birch trees on the West Meadow. Hundreds of these noisy birds fill the sky at dusk throughout the year.

[Overleaf] The south front of Kenwood House overlooks the Pasture Ground.

Kestrels can be seen year round in all parts of the Heath but favour the open grasslands and fields. They hunt from tree branches perched high over scrub on the lookout for mice and other prey scurrying on the ground below. Sometimes they will hover directly above their prey before swooping down, with their talons outstretched, to secure a meal.

Unpredictable flight patterns make it difficult to anticipate movement when photographing kestrels. This one launched from a tree in Pryors Field and hovered just a few metres from the lens.

[Left] A kestrel's diet consists mainly of small mammals and birds. On this occasion one can be seen pulling worms from the mud in Pryors Field.

[Right] Kestrels can see in the ultraviolet light range, allowing them to detect urine trails of small mammals around burrows, giving them the upper hand when searching for their favourite prey. Here a kestrel makes short work of a bank vole.

[Left] A male kestrel perching on an oak tree in Pryors Field. Male and female kestrels can be distinguished by their colour and size. An adult male has a grey head; females tend to be larger.

[Right] Kestrels have remarkably keen eyesight. This bird launched from a perch and caught a small worm from over 100 metres away.

[Overleaf] A kestrel and crow engage in an aerial battle. Birds of prey are often mobbed by crows, magpies and gulls although in this instance the kestrel has the upper hand, chasing the crow away. Shooting with a fast shutter speed against a blank sky allowed for crisp silhouettes of the two birds.

[Left] Wildlife watching people. A kestrel pauses momentarily on a low branch close to Hampstead No. 1 Pond.

[Overleaf] In 1767, former Prime Minister William Pitt the Elder lived in a mansion on Sandy Heath which was demolished in 1952. This structure, known as Pitt's Arch, is all that remains.

Lime Avenue is one of Hampstead Heath's most recognisable walkways. Flanked by a parallel row of lime trees, the avenue can be a busy place for commuters, children heading to and from school, runners and dog walkers. In autumn the bright yellow and green leaves join together in the canopy creating a tunnel that bursts with colour. Approximately a quarter of the trees in this row were replanted after the Great Storm of October 1987.

[Right] The distinctive autumnal yellow leaves of the lime tree stand out on an overcast misty morning.

[Overleaf] Lime Avenue, looking south-west towards East Heath Road. Soft, hazy sunlight from the east highlights the bark of a few trees helping give depth to the picture.

[Previous spread] A selection of leaves that can be seen on the Heath. [Left page, from top left] Nettle; yew; horse chestnut; oak; holly; wild service; elder; swan's neck thyme moss; dock. [Previous spread, right page, from top left] Ivy; bramble; cow parsley; broad buckler fern; hawthorn; beech; hornbeam; privet; Scots pine.

[Left] A mallard lifts its head from the water after feeding in one of the pools on Sandy Heath. This less-visited part of the Heath sits west of Spaniards Road and is at its most beautiful in the autumn. Colours reflected in the water merge with the background; the shallow depth of field effect is achieved with a telephoto lens.

[Right] Light bursts through the canopy close to the Vale of Health Pond. The strong highlights and dark shadows in this scene meant shooting a number of different exposures and selecting the most evenly balanced shot between light and dark.

[Overleaf] Low autumn light picks out the fiery yellows and reds in the canopy of a beech tree on the path to Bird Bridge.

PHOTOGRAPHER'S NOTES

'Take nothing but pictures, leave nothing but footprints.'

I saw this signpost many times during my travels in eastern and southern African national parks 17 years ago. I liked the simple message and kept it in mind on future travels to wilderness areas around the world. Every time I leave the Heath after a day of photographing I feel a buzz of excitement, hoping I've captured something special. Whether it's the flight of a kestrel, a sunset over Parliament Hill or a flowering field in spring with the backdrop of a stormy sky I hope I've taken away a collection of photographic treats in my camera bag and all I've left behind are footprints.

I've been visiting Hampstead Heath since my childhood and today I spend hours wandering there and honing my photography skills. It is a place where I can breathe fresh air and engage with nature in the heart of the city. I wanted to uncover some of the Heath's secret spots and hidden gems. To explore off the beaten track to find alternative routes and hopefully something new and intriguing to photograph. As I gathered fresh images I began to realise that here, in this great metropolis, stands a green space of extraordinary diversity.

Having grown up near to the Heath, I thought I knew the area well. However, after four years photographing nature here, I still feel like I've only scratched the surface. There are many species not covered in this book that play a crucial role in the Heath's ecosystem, but I had to stop somewhere and I have left a lifetime's worth of images behind.

No single picture can truly represent just how special Hampstead Heath is, nor can a book do its beauty and diversity justice. To produce powerful images and really grasp the character of a place takes time and I have learnt over the years that revisiting locations over and over again is the best way to achieve this. It is my mission to really understand the area and shine a light on it in a new way.

I hope this book inspires you to view your local green space in a new way. And above all, to take time to explore and appreciate the beauty of nature on your doorstep.

— Matthew Maran, London, 2016

A great crested grebe chick catches a ride on the back of an adult. Young will ride on the back of the parents for around ten days after hatching.

ACKNOWLEDGEMENTS

Photographing wildlife and landscapes is largely solitary work, but putting a book together is the complete opposite and very much a team effort. I've been lucky to collaborate with many talented, creative professionals and friends who have supported me not only throughout the making of this book but since my career began 16 years ago.

Heartfelt thanks to Rowena, your love, generosity, support and incredible hard work is forever appreciated.

To my family who I love and feel great love from. It gives me such confidence and helps me to pursue my dreams.

So much of the content for this book is down to the generosity, support and access provided by the City of London Corporation staff. Ecologist Adrian Brooker has worked on the Heath for 20 years. His knowledge of the fauna and flora was invaluable for capturing many images featured in the book. Many thanks to David Bentley for helping with my endless requests for special access. David Humphries and Conrad Daniels for the tree and fungi knowledge and getting me 30 metres up (and down) the old oak tree. Thanks to Paul Maskell whose love of the Heath is unrivalled. Big thanks to Terry Turner for access to the ponds, and lifeguards Mick Annegarn, Ian Campbell, Nicky Crowe, Dan Fawkes, Tony May, Wayne McBrien, Barry Nicholas, Tom Regan, Anderson Dos Santos and Greg Stechman for getting me to the other side of the pond and back.

Special thanks to David Brimble for your exemplary professionalism. Al Newman for the unparalleled attention to detail, you are a joy to work with. Many thanks to Imogen Green, Kate Smith, Iain Barratt and Sophie Smith at Catto Gallery for your generosity and support. Jane Fraser for listening and believing. Steve Swaby for the tight text edit and Frances de la Tour for the lovely foreword and support over the years. Josh Kempinski for helping with the image selection. Jessie Simmons for the lens loan which made the front cover. Craig Humphreys, one of these days I'll get my own 70-200mm. Jack Baker and Tom Hancock for the beautiful soundtrack to the film and Emile Kelly for making the film. Dave Vigay, Vick de Rijke, Will Vinson and Jo Lawry for your all-round love and support.

Also many thanks to Tim Aldred, The Baker Family, Craig Barnes, Sam Boffey, Danny Brooks, Eddie Ephraums, Anna Bonita Evans, Meg Game, Helen Gilks, Ben Gillett, Simon Glover, Tim Harris, Tony and Sharon Heald, Andreas Hobyan, Walti and Moni Huber, Corene Inouye, Simon Lee, Rachelle Macapagal Morris, Jeff Mitchum, Jason Niles, Marina and Piers Nimmo, Grace Rawnsley, Alex Reddicliffe, Chris Ryan, Rachel Smart, Chau Nguyen Tang, Graham Turner, Daniel Vogel, Kim Walker, Bob Warnock, Steve Watkins, Nathan and Lulu Watts, David Whistance, Alexander Muspratt-Williams, Rachel Wyndham Wincott, Mei Tak Yeh, Benj Youngson, Natasha Zlobec. City of London Corporation, Dawkins Colour, East German Ladies Swimming Team, English Heritage, Nature Picture Library, Outdoor Photography Magazine.

A big thank you to all those who contributed to the Kickstarter campaign, your generous backing made the printing of this book possible.

Liz and Øyvind Aamli, Jenifer Aird, John and Judith Aldersey-Williams, Nicholas Aleksander, Jim Allchin, Chris and Stephen Aparicio, Sandra Armor, Latoya Austin, Harry Thomas Kane Baker, Jack Baker, Sally and Rick Baker, Craig Barnes, Isobel Baron, Sarah Beal, Penelope Beavan, Rolf Behringer, Robert Benson, Niall Benvie, Jo Bergman, Todd and Liz Berman, Pierre-Yves Bernasconi, Carl Beuster, Beth Bevan, Jay Bevan, Matthew Biggs, Caroline Bittar, Jenny Blackwell, Norman Blair, Mary Block, Marco Bogliolo, Andrew Bound, Chakriya Bowman, Anne Marie Brady, Nicola Brathwaite, Elizabeth Bray, Tom Brent, Elizabeth Brown, Jennifer M. Brown, Jane Brunner, Fern Bryant, Rebecca Bryant and Christopher Gollop, Dan Burgess, Jules and Cheryl Burns, Peter Cairns, Matt Carlton, Jean Carroll, Anthony Casingena, Anna Caute, Jason Challen, The Chapman Family, Magash and Elisabeth Chetty, Brian Chia, Daniel Chinn, David and Nili Chinn, Matt Clark, Julie Claydon, Lawrence Cleary, Julia Cleverdon, Eleanor Coleman, Matthew J Coleman, Trevor Coleman, Tony's Continental, Philip Contini, Russell Conway, Diana E Cook, Dougal Corden, Yolanda Corden, Dianne Cornes, Alexandra Cornish, Nadia Costanzo, Katherine, Oli, Iris and Rowan Court, Helen Coyle, Fiona Cristante, Simon Crow, Caroline Dale, Olivia Daly, Jonne Damhuis, Barbara Davey, Chris Davis, Kerri Docherty, Tara Doherty, Tom Dullage, Kay and Robin Dunn, Len Dunne (EGLST), Michael Dunning, Peter Durbin, Nigel East, Christina Elmes, Tim Elwell, Tom Enraght-Moony, Stefan Estie, Philippa Fawcett, Alexandre Ferré, Joerg Fickenscher, Colin Finch, Emily and Andrew Finch, Danny Fitzgerald, Michelle and Cyril Flajsner, Jeremy and Mel Foster, Fozia and Lorenzo, Jeremy Franks, Jane Fraser, Peter Freeman, Steve Friendship, David F. Gallagher, Cherie Garrett, Stephen Gibbon, Pat Gibson, Helen Gilks, Wayne Giza, Colin Gleeson, Kitty Gleeson, Judith Glover, Simon Glover, Gray Golka, Alex Gordon, Chris and John Gormley, Candy Gourlay, Kate Grange and Charlie Cory-Wright, Martin, Michelle and Lucy Gray, Johanna Green, Judy Griggs, Kevin Gundle, Katie and Mike Gurden, Daniel Hahn, Roger and Nuala Hancock, Thomas Hancock, John Hannah, Jonathan and Jennifer Harris, Natalie Harvey, Joan and Larry Hatheway, Michelle Hayes, Sharon and Tony Heald, Paula Hedderson, Shirlie Hemmings-Portas, Thomas Heueisen, Marion Hill, Helen Hodge, Kaitlyn Hogue Mellini, Gerard Holbrook, Georgia Holderness, Laurens Holve, Alexander Howden, D. Howell, Walti Huber, Karren Hughes, Keren M. Humphrey, Craig and Sandy Humphreys, Peter Humphreys, Rowena Humphreys, Francis Hur, Marc Hutchinson, Jonathan Hyer, Roser Icart, Lisa Young In, Mike Ingleheart, Jamie's Whaling Station Tofino BC, Christopher Jenkins, Hoang Anh Jenkins, Paul and Joey, Samantha and Jonathan Johncox, Nick Jordan, CK Joshi (EGLST), Veronica and Stan Judd, Katja Ulanoswki, Victoria Keith, Josh Kempinski, Peter Kenyatta, Sara Khoyratty, Sally King, Ruth Kirsh, Jeremy Koreski, Vassilis Koulovassilopoulos, Geoff Lamb, Dr Renée LaScala, Geoffroy Laviolette and Isabella di Carpegna, Jo Lawry, Peter Layton, Sarah Layton, Elizabeth Lazou, Martin Ledigo, Toby Leigh, Josh Leuner, Baptiste Leurent, Beattie Lewis, Kate Lewis, Vic Lewis, Dave Lidwell, Louise and Kay Lieber, Evelin Longo, Martyn Loughran, Winona LoveBlossom, Robin Lustig and Ruth Kelsey, Josh Lustig, Kathy MacEwen, Colleen Mahaney, Jason Mais and Tim Webb, Simon, Irina, Mia and Daniel Malynicz, Lucy Maran, Michael Maran, Sue Maran, Toni Marcus, Rachelle Marie Macapagal Morris, Patrick McAnerney, Helen and Barrie McClennon, Sam McCombe, Eugene McConville, Fergal McEntee, Francis McInerny, Maggie McKenzie, Fiona Mcswein, Rod Mearing, Robert Meekings, Lauren Elizabeth Miller, Liz Millner, Adam Moore, Jesse Morley, Rachel Moses, Sally Mumford, The Murray-Burrows Family, Alex Muspratt-Williams, Deborah Mylonas, Paul Mylrea (EGLST), Kristina Neoushoff, Dan Newman, Nicole and Xavier Nicolas, Marina Nimmo, Ronald Olufunwa, Richard Owen, Mary Elizabeth Paddock, Deborah Pancheri Wallace, Sarah Paterson, Stuart Paterson, Colleen Patrick-Goudreau, Peter Pearse, Stephanie Pemberton, Mathieu Pendergast, Oliver Perritt, Giampiero Pesenti, Philip Petrou, Phage, Dan Phillips, Vanessa Pike, Yuko and Rayner Pitt, Andrew Plaistowe, Dwight and Kirsten Poler, Tibor Poor, Molly Price, Nicky and John Price, Oliver Pudney, Dr Quack, Harriet Radley, Matthew and Emma Rea, Lisa Reading, Amy Reams, Alexander Reddicliffe, Kathy Reddington, Brighde Reed and Seb Ranger, Ivis Reed Bohlen, Lee Renee, Melissa and Alberto Revel-Chion, Caryl Rey, Hilary Reynolds, Teresa Reynolds, Jilayne Rickards, Andrew Robins and Tasha Arnold, Max Robinson, Nev Robinson, Sam Robinson, Lauren Rood and Tony Joseph, Deborah Rookes, Steve and Celia Rosenbaum, Umberto Rota, Tim Russell (EGLST), Jenny Russell, Morena and Paul Russell, Kamil Rybka, Adam Sanders, Ross Saxby, Martin Schlote, Nicholas Schoeder, Janine Scoggins, Peter Scott, Jay Seabrook, Agnes Segal, Mike Segal, Sheena Shah, Rowena Sheppard, Tatyana Shynkarenko, Allan Siddick, Matt Siddick, Jo Simister, Jessie Simmons, Mathilde Simmons, Jeremy Simons, Anne Simpson, Rachel Singer, Sue and Keith Singer, Rachel Smart, Karen and Mark Smith, Mike Smith, Sophie Smith, Juliette Sonabend, Angela Sorkin, Amber Sorrell, Harriet Spicer, Heather Spicer, Adrian Squirrell, Elliot Stillman, Anthony Stoll, Strittmatter Family, Mike Struik, Rob Stubbs, Greta Stults, Rachel Sturgis, Louise Sturt, Coriander Stuttard, Julie Takasaki, Nufar and Yaron Tal, Tammy, Vinnie, Celeste and Luca, Ben Tarling, Mathieu Testud, Hewer Text, Christopher Tjiattas, Andy de la Tour, Sarah Towle, Dr April Nunes Tucker, Alex Turner, Graham Turner, Kimberley Turner, Eva Turrell, Vincent Valentin, Wilma van Heusden-Snoeren, Betty Varnava, Elizabeth Venn, Chris Veys, Dave Vigay, Ute Villavicencio, Charlotte Vinken, Bronwen Vinson, Mary Vinson, Daniel Vogel, Sherri Voigt, Martin Wadlow, Sir John and Lady Waite, Kim Walker, Jackie Wastell, Sophie Waterhouse, Nicola Waterman, Nathan Watts, Sally Weintrobe, Claire Wellings, Rick Wells, John Weston and Rachel Lord, Nigel and Sue Wheatley, Julian Wheeler, John Wilkinson, Andrea Williams, Charlotte Wiseman, Linda and Peter Wiseman, Pawel Wisniowski, Susi Wooldridge, Julie Woods, Matthew Wootliff, Rachel Wyndham Wincott, Henry Wyn-Jones, Mei Tak Yeh, Denise Yoko Berndt, Marcus Yorke, Doug Young.

ALSO FROM HEMISPHERE PUBLISHING AND MATTHEW MARAN PHOTOGRAPHY

A selection of large-format diasec-mounted panoramic prints are available from Catto Gallery, Hampstead, London. cattogallery.co.uk

Vancouver Island, Barkley to Clayoquot by Matthew Maran (Hemisphere Publishing, 2011)

Vancouver Island, Barkley to Clayoquot with limited-edition hand-made cedar case and photographic print

Matthew Maran Photography Hampstead Heath greetings cards